embodied

Kayla Collingwood

embodied

©2022 by Kayla Collingwood
www.kaylacollingwood.com
contact@kaylacollingwood.com

Cover design ©2022 by Kayla Collingwood

ISBN 978-2-9584762-0-5

contents

contents

Anticipation

The twinkling
of twilight
gives me
an inkling
of your being
imminently
invading
the evening.

I am feeling
a sunrise
arriving,
caressing,
disarming me,
increasing
the desire
you're inspiring.

Hidden Worlds

Just beneath the ocean's surface
lie one thousand hidden worlds,
just waiting to be discovered
by a daring adventurer.
Could there be traces of Atlantis,
or a shipwreck long forgotten,
or unopened treasure chests,
telling ancient stories?
I remain in the shallows,
so I will not lose my breath;
I keep the shore in sight,
and let my mind wander.

In Harmony

The prism through which you see the world
contains a spectrum of analogous hues
when compared with my own colour wheel,
adding a palette of shades to what I already knew.
You place your hands on my shoulders,
indicating gently and whispering intimately
about all the details and symbols I should observe
as I succumb to sumptuous scenes out of curiosity.
Mystical, potent music fills the twilight air;
the sound of Pan's flute seduces sweet Syrinx,
harmonic layers intensify the soundscape,
and I understand how our souls came to be linked.

Daybreak

Softly the light breaks through the night,
touches your eyes, dreaming, closed tight.
I hear you breathe,
and I can't believe
that you're mine.

What do you see in your fantasies?
Is it me, dancing through your dreams?
When the day breaks
and I see your face,
I have peace.

I sit, tranquil, by the windowsill,
drinking my fill of early morning still.
Black coffee scent,
your soft accent -
live, I will.

Tongue

The rhythm of your words,
produced by the percussion of your lips,
keeps time with the beat of your heart.

I can only dream of creating
such crafted, complex music;
no mastery of mechanisms - maladroite.

I listen to your discourse, mesmerised,
discovering new worlds
given breath by your tongue,
and understanding life a little more.

Your music now has meaning,
where once I heard only mystical chanting,
relegated to ancient folklore.

Stay

Intertwined,
two strands of life's weaving
rest loosely,
untied.

I sense my own breathing
while I feel
your heartbeat, awakening
my soul
as it heals,
and my body is shaking -
with what?

Several sentiments, not yet understood,
not by me,
and not by those who really should
understand.

But who am I to expect
the answer
when I can
barely comprehend the question:
do I stay?

Secret Path

Take me down the secret path
that only the lovers know,
where everything glows
in the light of a scented candle.
The air is filled with vanilla and musk;
my tongue flavour-laced,
combined with your taste,
creating a sensory phenomenon.

Closer

Draw a little closer,
succumb to the electric pull;
break in and lean into my circle -
let me feel your presence in full.

Breathe through your emotions;
rest your forehead on mine.
Let our parted lips collide
as you look deep into my eyes.

Desiderium

In a Devil's hour hypnopompic delusion,
involuntarily I call out your name,
before succumbing once again to slumber.

Night and day, blue devils haunt my dreams.
Every time you are the protagonist;
I have lost count of the exact number.

For you, my reason, I am lost for words:
you gifted me Sehnsucht and saudade,
and more than language can describe.

Visit me again, do not hide your presence;
give me some respite from my agitation,
salved by a brief glimpse of your eyes.

Missing

I have been collecting fragments
of faded memories made with you;
I placed them in an ivory box,
decorated with mother-of-pearl details.
I have been repeating meaningful phrases
from songs shared with you;
I store the rhythms in my body,
and the melodies in my soul.
I have been reminiscing
over photographs that I remembered to take;
my greatest wish, my deepest longing
is to once again see your face.
I have been remembering
how it feels to be held in your strong arms;
in my dreams you are present
and you pull me into your sweet embrace.

Wait

The Elysian Fields glisten in the distance,
catching my eye with their golden promises.
I begin to run; I know the right direction,
but the path is overgrown with ancient roses.
Strong arms hold me back as I leave the starting block,
and a voice reprimands gently in firm undertones,
reminding me that I must keep on working steadily,
for the nettles must be stripped from the cobbled stones,
before I can reach the end of this silent path
that I alone chose. Even though Time has decided
the day and the hour that I must proceed;
I must follow her lead and consent to be guided.
The way must be cleared if what is to come
is to be mine when the chest at last lies before me;
while I wait I am tearing down all the barbed barriers,
and learning the skills to forge my skeleton key.
One day I will be awoken in the middle of the night,
prepared for battle, but still a little frightened.
Patience knows well just what is required,
and bestows the gifts and the tools of enlightenment.

Attention

A goddess, I am floating
glowing, golden, serene
in the blue-flamed void
between real and surreal.
Fire burns in your eyes
as you fix upon my frame,
with an uncontrollable desire
which words cannot explain.
Yet you take your time
and restrain your passion,
lest you should be lost
in futile desperation.
You give in to the magnetism,
and I relish your attention,
basking in sweet triumph
as I reach a timeless dimension.

Dangerous Game

I played it safe,
kept my cool,
held my tongue,
stuck to the rules.

I felt your breath -
heart beat out of time.
You took my hand,
guiding me out of the lines.

I flirted with danger,
knowing all too well
that I would soon fall
under your spell.

You drove wild
what once was tame,
and now I'm here playing
a dangerous game.

Moonglade

The pale moonglade
leads me to you -
an elusive treasure,
like the pot of gold
at the end of a rainbow.
I sit on the shore,
observing sea ripples;
the shimmering light
reflecting the fluttering
of this anguished heart.
If only the moonglade
were a solid path -
then I could stumble
over the ocean,
in search of you.
But I am on the shore,
constrained by gravity,
so I transmit my love
telepathically,
hoping you will know.

3 A.M.

Like a thief in the night,
you escaped from my dreams,
where I held you secure
for your own safety.

Like a seaside vision
you appeared on the horizon,
lighting up the night,
awakening my senses.

Like forbidden fruit,
tantalisingly sweet,
you were irresistible
as I drew you to my lips.

Like a hallucination,
your likeness materialising,
then just as soon dissipating -
were you ever here?

White Room

My footsteps echo terribly, carried by cathedral acoustics
as I pace with determination in your general direction.
Light pours through the panes, illuminating my path,
glowing so glaringly pure that it nearly blinds me.
Marbled floors shine, as though they were freshly polished
in preparation for this moment, reflecting the surrounding silence.
I fraternise with your eyes and send a message telepathically,
channelling my intrinsic boldness, hinting at the power I hold.
Are you afraid of my strength, my cool resolve and calm exterior,
the door behind which one thousand worlds can be found?
I stand before you cautiously, studying your radiant disguise;
we know well what lies beneath, immortalised in that white room.

Presence

I catch a waft of your cologne -
my surroundings suddenly fade away
as I find myself wrapped in your arms,
and for a transient, transcendent moment,
I migrate to those perfect days,
where I am alive again.
I hear your voice whispering my name,
or is it a cruel trick of the breeze,
fervently promising your presence,
as if you were in the vicinity -
is this fate or a fateful scheme?
Perhaps in another life.

Prologue

The first chord rises
out of expectant silence,
and a melody gently forms
under your fingers
as you shift across
the four strings.
This is our first meeting,
the twisting beginning.

Later, your hands have found mine.
I feel the calluses on your fingertips
as I study their designs -
holding them tenderly
and gazing at their intricacy.
I fall into your striking eyes;
I am not accustomed
to someone of such beauty.

I suddenly lose control
and am no longer my own,
seeking to devour and to be devoured
by this passion that began burning
over the passing hours.
I place your hands on my skin
until I lose all sense of where I end and you begin.

In the morning light,
you hold me with strength and tenderness combined,
and whisper life while I slumber,
holding on to the last moment of my dreams,
waking to the wonder
who sleeps beside me.

Without You

I am sitting here alone,
feeling the winter wind caress my cheeks,
tinted pink from the icy chill,
brought to me by polar sources.
I dedicate each breath to you,
and I am filled with inexplicable power
which only thoughts of you can inspire,
and only your love can replete.
If only a hologram were generated,
drawing on mystical waves and forces
so I could see you here beside me,
just as beautiful as I can remember,
seemingly real as long as I do not attempt
to reach out and touch you.
Your presence seems to dissipate
in the fading light of the twilight hour;
I gasp for air as I lose our connection,
and to a deep sense of loss I surrender.
There is nothing more to say:
my world is not the same without you.

Language

Deftly selected,
appropriately seductive,
artfully playful
phrases,
gently triggering
erogenous zones -
mental stimulus
points.

Fallen Woman

I climbed out of a shallow pit,
accepting my fall from grace;
I walked into my freedom,
putting on my bravest face.
My authority was to another
the greatest sin one could commit -
to reign, the single gravest crime
when the order was to submit.
I held the keys to my fortune,
and I unlocked the prison gate,
strolled into my gallery of jewels,
and took hold of my estate.
I relived my coronation,
as I sat upon my throne;
my rightful place, my inheritance,
my responsibility alone.
There are those who criticise,
who plot my downfall and my death,
but it is these same devious schemers
who devised this evil mess.
I may no longer be innocent,
yet I am far from criminal;
I am a daughter of infamous Eve:
born to be original.

Vanitas

You peel back the layers
surrounding my soul
with such luxurious ease,
it is frightening.
Suddenly I am faced
with a silvery mirror,
reflecting Picasso fragments -
harsh enlightening.
How did you know
just where to find
all my concealed pieces
and collate them all,
revealing faded faces,
echoes of vagrant ghosts,
wistful, cubist memories
and angry, black scrawls?
You tell me my desires,
with careful brushstrokes,
caressing the edges
of each component.
I disassemble in your arms,
prepared to be your muse,
to revel in revered vanity
in this blissful moment.

There's something about you

There's something about you
that makes me lose all rationality:
you invade my mind and take it over,
and I'm lost in the thoughts you elicit.
I never saw myself
as someone who could be so wild and free,
but when you delve beneath my composure,
I'll willingly give anything you solicit.
Maybe I made a few mistakes,
and someday they'll return to haunt me,
but if my errors land me in your arms,
I'd regret it if prudence caused me to miss it.

Trance

25

I lie in solitude, alone with my darkest thoughts,
in an agitated arena where fire and ice have met,
and I am confronted by my deepest desires,
unfulfilled here in my cold and desolate bed.

I lie here patiently, waiting for your imminent arrival,
hoping you can satisfy my wild and ravenous soul,
with your strong, steady arms and gratifying eyes,
as our shadows struggle zealously for control.

I lie in hypnagogic trance, drifting into peaceful dreams,
where every need is met and our souls are one,
where programmed provocations have vanished from sight,
and all tensions and frustrations are coming undone.

Temporary Lover

Days turned to weeks into months into a year,
and I am yet to see signs that the end is near,
yet I know that someday our love will come to a close,
and maybe we will never speak again - who knows?
For the moment, we just find that we are crazy for each other;
all I want is to know every last inch of my temporary lover.
In the back of my mind I wonder when the time will come,
when we'll sever the tie because we want to find "the one",
but I stubbornly retreat back into my inspired imagination
because I'm unwilling to accept that there's a date of expiration.
Will it catch us unawares? maybe it will be expected,
but whatever the case, our worlds will be fractured,
and deep within our souls, hidden well below the surface,
we'll find love bites and long nights and permanent bruises.

Love At First Sight

My mind was absorbed in a watercolour world,
far from the poisoned arrows of reality,
when you caught my eye and my soul began to swirl;
is this love or some strange kind of malady?
Time stopped and the hustle faded into a mist,
as I noticed my hastening respiration.
I wondered how my heart might feel to be kissed
by this vision, Adonis' apparition.
Then I walked on my way and vibrant was the sky,
and the flora was magically painted.
Will I see you again, will you be part of my life;
could we someday become acquainted?

Flames

You are in my thoughts
more frequently than I care to admit;
as night returns, so too do our secrets,
hidden from the brightness
of the sunlight.

I need a dose of you
to take the edge off the craving
which has been eating incessantly
at me all day.

I am here alone,
yet you have found a way to be present;
you are setting my body and soul on fire,
and I long to taste your kisses
as the flames ignite.

Can you feel the heat
as it permeates the air?
I gaze at you fervently;
draw near.

Boy

You're young and you're sweet,
and you know what you do to me,
telling me daring things, softly whispering
bedroom secrets on repeat.
When you first held me to your heart,
in your embrace at once I felt
somehow you're less of a mess than I was
with the same years under your belt.
Despite your tender youth,
you've lived a little bit of life;
since you're in my head and in my bed,
you must be doing something right.
For now we're driven by hunger;
we feast until we get our fill,
but will we still burn with desire
with adult responsibilities and bills?
Maybe life's burdens
will become too heavy to hold,
you're probably here for fun and you're not the one,
so let's just put on the blindfold.

Free

The gate clangs shut, metal on metal,
as I am herded from the sky to the earth
by invisible forces and their assistants.
I search for the forest through steel bars,
longing to live among the mysteries
held within its cool pine expanses.
I struggle to see beyond the trees,
but I make out the shimmering sea,
and I hear a comforting voice calling me.
Will I hear the key turn, will I be released,
will the fetters someday be removed from my feet?
My life's ambition, my heart's dream, is to be free.

Unpacking

I heave this heavy load
on the ground,
and a violent echo
shakes all around.
It has been on my back
for an eternal minute,
and I never knew
that I could remove it.
I pull out the contents,
one by one,
analysing each item
until the task is done.
I clean what I can,
polishing the brass,
and I collect each piece
of broken glass,
finding some in my skin -
how did it catch me there? -
finding all the lost relics
I was forced to share.
Some unlabeled tins,
should I need something reliable;
it's time to throw away
the falsely paradisiacal.
Once all is unpacked
and sorted painfully through,
I reorganise what remains,
and walk on with you.

The Present Moment

Put aside your mind and float
away to foreign lands.
The daily work is over now -
night takes you in her hands.
She leads you to the isle of dreams,
where trials of life aren't found -
deep into your inner soul,
through tunnels underground.
Escape into the ether
and remember who you are.
The other voices are not heard;
they menace from afar.
Don't look in their direction;
they do not dare come near,
for silence is the emperor -
the only ruler here.
When morning comes, so too comes hope;
sweet moments float in time,
waiting to be gathered in
and set down in your mind.
Nestle in the collarbone
of little victories,
building up a scrapbook
filled with precious memories.

Flight

The clouds drift low in the winter sky,
with no direction of their own,
pushed by the wind past the contrail lines,
streaking white where the 'planes have flown.

I watch as they glide from my vantage point -
stable, resting on the ground,
wishing I moved as they, but my frozen joints
hold me still; tight with ice I am bound.

The sun's rays pour down through the foggy haze,
showing me somewhere bathed in light,
and when spring comes again to lengthen the days,
I'll be poised, my wings readied for flight.

Secrets

Deftly unfasten what holds
textiles tightly over my skin,
and let the fabric float to the floor
as I breathe you in.
Softly whisper what has lingered
idling invisibly in dust particles,
held unbearably unspoken until
we surmounted the obstacles.
Swiftly unravel every thread
sewn scrupulously in my soul;
layers of life and fractured love
formed a delicate tableau.
Dauntlessly explore my
bareskin being under the moonlight,
found vulnerable once again,
but this time it feels right.

Lenses

They offer you their lenses,
to filter the streams of colour
blazing in your direction,
so that you might see more clearly.
You press them into your eyes,
not questioning the giver,
fearing the effects of the view,
should you ever want to see.
A child falls motionless by the wall,
built to divide, infused with hate -
two perpetrators, one accused,
condemned by a crosshair target.
There is war everywhere, they say,
but we only want peace, they say,
as another bomb explodes at our feet,
planted by those offering lip-service.
You see snapshots and curated images,
hear the cries of the chosen ones,
while the hidden puppeteers continue
pulling the strings of the marionettes.
The lens wearer has been desensitised,
transformed by years of erosion;
silently and willingly we all fall captive
to those who only want to hurt us.

Obsession

You are a consensual obsession,
not an unhealthy addiction;
I long for you to teach me
those one thousand sweet lessons.
You tell me you're on your way
to show me what I'm missing,
and my mind lights up, struck
with thoughts of us kissing.
I can close the door softly,
say goodbye whenever I please,
but tonight I left it open,
so you can enter my dreams.

Cosmos

Soft, ambient sounds accompany the most awesome of visions;
a deep, ombré sky where rich shades of violet and blue collide,
speckled with cherished wishes and prayers, as loved ones
look curiously down upon us with their distant, abstract smiles.

There is a peaceful, appreciable aura surrounding you;
it beguiles me, like a powerful, irresistible silver magnet.
You draw music from the depths of the mystical great beyond,
absorbing its true essence, and harnessing its magic.

I have lost all sense of control, yet I am far from frightened;
the universe has whispered to me, and the stars have aligned.
Beneath the heavens I peer past the bright reflections in your eyes
searching for the secrets which I'm sure that they must hide.

Your touch sends shivers like shockwaves through my skin;
your energy courses through me, rocketing like a meteor.
Under the spectacular open sky our souls combine with a kiss;
a spell is cast, and through the tranquil atmosphere we soar.

Nymph

Like a forest nymph, earthy and wise,
I stretch out my fingers to connect to arboreal forces,
summoning me to seek the magical sources
of this sacred land.

I am lured by a song - ancient, inspired -
by a magnetism stronger than anything I've ever known,
and a pure light is emitted from my ring of moonstone
as I touch your hand.

Calathea

A stripy calathea
ornaments a cosy corner
of Scandinavian books.
Blush pink lattés
fade into the décor:
the perfect photographic look.
An almond cappuccino
smoulders on a square table,
caffeine fuel for an artist.
Uncertainties are lost
in a jungle of coffee
and murmurs and laughter.

Rose

She displays her crimson petals,
blushing under the enamoured gaze
which appreciates her arresting beauty
in the light of late afternoon sun.
She belongs to no one but nature -
Flora's daughter; a calm presence
drawing attention without effort
with her divine, resplendent essence.
When Rosalia comes around,
she is the season's diamond entry;
in splendid dress she elegantly waltzes,
unmatched, unfazed object of envy.

Lily

Five hundred years old, this musty room,
where many a pair have said "I do":
today an anxious bride and a fidgeting groom,
with his silver cufflinks and sterling in her shoe.

Adorning the wooden table is a crystal vase,
filled with fresh-cut lilies, picked by loving hands,
accompanied by seven-armed candelabras in brass,
with dripping white candles, nearing the pans.

The festivities begin, in the venerable hall,
where the walls are covered with tapestries and art -
Pyramus and Thisbe at the centre of them all -
star-crossed lovers surveying wedded sweethearts.

Garden

In deep beds sleep colours - green and rainbows -
awaiting the sun's warmth and the sky's opening,
to unfurl like threatened cobras, rising like phoenixes,
soaring like symphonies in spring's replenishing.

One day in the early morning - fresh and frosty -
sprouts will cautiously peek out into the wild,
then later will come children, inspired and ravenous,
harvesting what the garden generously provides.

I know enough

I know enough now to know how little I know,
and to know that what is touched by the light
may hide a different story deep down below.
I've seen enough exploitation of diligent good intent
to know that those flashing the most charming smiles
can create the same poverty they have the power to prevent.
I've held enough manifestations of pain in my arms
to know that dark thoughts expressed one too many times
can turn harmless red flags into violently screeching alarms.
I've heard enough "'til death do us part" vows engraved
on silence; seen enough hearts fragmented, barely alive
to know that death may not only be found in a grave.

Promise

Shards of broken promises perforated the native plain,
fences and walls were built to deter intruders,
yet the worst offenders were our protectors.
One promise stood strong: an unfaltering defender,
demanding only trust, offered us the answer.
Someday this place will be renewed and whole again.

Overture

Navy clouds part like curtains and reveal a pale moon;
its light shines through the open shutters,
and we are hit by a spotlight as we take centre stage.

Your chest is illuminated, mixed with patches of gloom;
my eyes hunger, my heart is set a-flutter,
my fingers trace your skin, like a parchment page.

You are my muse, all that matters in this room;
I hang on your every breath, and every sound uttered
as our fingers interlock and our souls engage...

Graphite

Your fingers trace a graphite outline -
the carefully-crafted sketch of an artist
planning each stroke of inspired design,
on a blank canvas of delicate skin.

Highlights, shadows, and shades -
favourite features accentuated and defined,
drawing out the magnificent details
stored in your labyrinthine mind.

Flow

Legato and slow,
the music ebbs and flows
like gently foaming waves,
falling into time,
with a rhythm and a rhyme
underpinning every page.
We push and we pull,
resisting any rules,
yet succumbing in the end...
a little give and take,
leaving sparks in our wake,
wanting time to extend.
Tension and release,
balancing the sheets;
no time for respite.
Building up desire,
indulging in its fire,
burning splendid and bright.

Beloved

I am drawn to you
with such intensity
that I am sure that
something beyond me
is pulling the strings.
My only desire
is to feel your skin,
magnetised like my own,
our love interwoven
as I breathe you in.
Heaven, grant me
sweet emancipation
from the constraints
of sacred obligations,
of worldly expectations.
You are my freedom;
I will be your hiding place,
a rest for your weary head.
As our fingers interlace,
I've found home in your embrace.

My Home

In the incandescent light,
where my visions come to life,
where the world is left behind,
I am lost in easy dreams,
I indulge my fantasies,
and I lose all sense of time:
this is my home.

I wake and face the day -
has my soul passed away?
Am I still the same inside?
I don't recognise this place,
and I never saw that face;
I don't know how to survive -
where is my home?

Open Road

The curtains part and the sun peeks in;
I am bathed in light and the shadows scatter.
I glance at the time and sigh with relief,
because today the hour does not matter.
You gently brush my arm with your fingertips,
as if to see if our thoughts are synchronised:
let's leave this place for an undefined duration...
seconds of spontaneity flicker in my eyes.
Let's take to the open road this morning,
while we are not restricted by anyone or anything,
while we are young and free and unlimited,
and while shared company is still a pleasant thing.
A journey begins which has no planned destination,
and I smile at the freedom this offers sometimes.
You press play and music fills the silence we enjoyed;
the road stretches before us with no end in sight.

Embodied

I needed to know you
in order to know love,
in order to know myself,
in order to weave stories
from the tangible traces
held in international museums,
held on ancient pages,
held in long-lost diaries.
You are my muse,
the inspiration for my art,
the inspiration for my spirit,
the inspiration for my life.
I channel your lessons
through my soul,
through my body,
until I am made whole.

end